July 2012

INFORMATION SECURITY

Environmental Protection Agency Needs to Resolve Weaknesses

GAO
Accountability * Integrity * Reliability
Highlights

Highlights of GAO-12-696, a report to congressional requesters

INFORMATION SECURITY

Environmental Protection Agency Needs to Resolve Weaknesses

Why GAO Did This Study

EPA is responsible for protecting human health and the environment by implementing and enforcing the laws and regulations intended to improve the quality of the nation's air, water, and lands. The agency's policies and programs affect virtually all segments of the economy, society, and government. In addition, it relies extensively on networked computer systems to collect a wealth of environmental data and to disseminate much of this information while also protecting other forms of sensitive or confidential information.

Because of the importance of the security of EPA's information systems, GAO was asked to determine whether the agency has effectively implemented appropriate information security controls to protect the confidentiality, integrity, and availability of the information and systems that support its mission. To do this, GAO tested security controls over EPA's key networks and systems; reviewed policies, plans, and reports; and interviewed officials at EPA headquarters and two field offices.

What GAO Recommends

GAO is making 12 recommendations to the Administrator of EPA to fully implement elements of EPA's comprehensive information security program. In commenting on a draft of this report, EPA's Assistant Administrator generally agreed with GAO's recommendations. Two of GAO's recommendations were revised to incorporate EPA's comments. In a separate report with limited distribution, GAO is also making 94 recommendations to EPA to enhance access and other information security controls over its systems.

View GAO-12-696. For more information, contact Gregory C. Wilshusen at (202) 512-6244 or wilshuseng@gao.gov or Dr. Nabajyoti Barkakati at (202) 512-4499 or barkakatin@gao.gov.

What GAO Found

Although the Environmental Protection Agency (EPA) has taken steps to safeguard the information and systems that support its mission, security control weaknesses pervaded its systems and networks, thereby jeopardizing the agency's ability to sufficiently protect the confidentiality, integrity, and availability of its information and systems. The agency did not fully implement access controls, which are designed to prevent, limit, and detect unauthorized access to computing resources, programs, information, and facilities. Specifically, the agency did not always (1) enforce strong policies for identifying and authenticating users by, for example, requiring the use of complex (i.e., not easily guessed) passwords; (2) limit users' access to systems to what was required for them to perform their official duties; (3) ensure that sensitive information, such as passwords for system administration, was encrypted so as not to be easily readable by unauthorized individuals; (4) keep logs of network activity or monitor key parts of its networks for possible security incidents; and (5) control physical access to its systems and information, such as controlling visitor access to computing equipment. In addition to weaknesses in access controls, EPA had mixed results in implementing other security controls. For example, EPA conducted appropriate background investigations for employees and contractors to ensure sufficient clearance requirements had been met before permitting access to information and information systems. However,

- EPA had not always securely configured network devices and updated operating system and database software with patches to protect against known vulnerabilities.

- EPA had not always ensured equipment used for sanitization and disposal of media was tested to verify correct performance.

An underlying reason for the control weaknesses is that EPA has not fully implemented a comprehensive information security program. Although EPA has established a framework for its security program, the agency has not yet fully implemented all elements of its program. Specifically, it did not always finalize policies and procedures to guide staff in effectively implementing controls; ensure that all personnel were given relevant security training to understand their roles and responsibilities; update system security plans to reflect current agency security control requirements; assess management, operational, and technical controls for agency systems at least annually and based on risk; and implement a corrective action process to track and manage all weaknesses when remedial actions were necessary. Sustained management oversight and monitoring are necessary for EPA to implement these key information security practices and controls. Until EPA fully implements a comprehensive security program, it will have limited assurance that its information and information systems are adequately protected against unauthorized access, use, disclosure, modification, disruption, or loss.

Contents

Abbreviations

ASSERT	Automated System Security Evaluation and Remediation Tracking
EPA	Environmental Protection Agency
FIPS	Federal Information Processing Standards
FISMA	Federal Information Security Management Act of 2002
IT	information technology
MTIPS	Managed Trusted Internet Protocol Services
NIST	National Institute of Standards and Technology
NSA	National Security Agency
OMB	Office of Management and Budget
POA&M	plan of action and milestones

July 19, 2012

Congressional Requesters

The Environmental Protection Agency's (EPA) mission is to protect human health and the environment by implementing and enforcing the laws and regulations intended to improve the quality of the nation's air, water, and lands. EPA's policies and programs affect virtually all segments of the economy, society, and government. In meeting its mission, the agency relies extensively on networked computer systems to collect a wealth of environmental data and to disseminate much of this information to the public while also protecting sensitive or confidential information.

Protection of mission-critical and sensitive information technology (IT) resources on information systems remains an ongoing challenge for EPA as federal agencies experience evolving and growing cyber attacks. Without a well-designed security program, EPA's information and information systems could be subject to unauthorized access, disclosure, disruption, modification, or destruction.

In response to your request, we evaluated EPA's information security program. Our objective was to determine whether EPA has effectively implemented appropriate information security controls to protect the confidentiality, integrity, and availability of the information and systems that support its mission.

To accomplish this objective, we examined computer security controls over EPA's network infrastructure and systems key to the agency's mission. We also examined information security policies, plans, and procedures; reviewed testing of controls over key applications; interviewed key agency officials; and reviewed EPA inspector general reports to identify previously reported weaknesses.

We conducted this performance audit from July 2011 to July 2012 in accordance with generally accepted government auditing standards. Those standards require that we plan and perform the audit to obtain sufficient, appropriate evidence to provide a reasonable basis for our findings and conclusions based on our audit objective. We believe that the evidence obtained provides a reasonable basis for our findings and conclusions based on our audit objective. See appendix I for a complete description of our objective, scope, and methodology.

Background

Safeguarding government computer systems and the sensitive information that resides on them is an ongoing challenge because of the complexity and interconnectivity of systems, the ease of obtaining and using hacking tools, the steady advances in the sophistication and effectiveness of attack technology, and the emergence of new and more destructive attacks. Without adequate safeguards, systems are vulnerable to individuals and groups with malicious intentions, who may obtain sensitive information, commit fraud, disrupt operations, or launch attacks against other computer systems and networks. Federal agencies have experienced a significant rise in security incidents in recent years, with data from the U.S. Computer Emergency Readiness Team showing an increase in security incidents and events from 29,999 in 2009 to 42,887 in 2011.

EPA Plays a Key Role in Protecting the Environment

EPA was established in 1970 in response to concerns about environmental pollution. To perform its statutory responsibilities, EPA develops and enforces regulations and gives grants to and sponsors partnerships with state environmental programs, non-profit organizations, educational institutions, and others. In addition, the agency conducts research and publishes materials on a variety of environmental topics.

In fiscal year 2011, EPA's appropriation was about $8.6 billion. The agency has headquarters in Washington, D.C., 10 regional areas, and multiple laboratories and centers that support research and development. At headquarters, EPA develops national programs, policies, and regulations for mission areas, as described in table 1.

Table 1: EPA Program Offices

Office	Responsibilities
Office of Air and Radiation	Oversees indoor and outdoor air quality, industrial air pollution, pollution from vehicles and engines, radon, acid rain, stratospheric ozone depletion, climate change, and radiation protection. Administers environmental laws related to these areas.
Office of Chemical Safety and Pollution Prevention	Works to protect the public and the environment from pesticides and toxic chemicals and to prevent pollution. Implements laws pertaining to these efforts.
Office of Enforcement and Compliance Assurance	Works with regional offices and partners with state and tribal governments and other federal agencies on civil and criminal enforcement that targets serious water, air, and chemical hazards.
Office of Environmental Information	Manages the life cycle of information to support EPA's mission of protecting human health and the environment. Responsible for the quality of EPA's information and the efficiency and reliability of EPA's technology, data collection and exchange efforts, and access services. Provides technology services and manages EPA's IT investments.

Office	Responsibilities
Office of International and Tribal Affairs	Works with experts from EPA's other program and regional offices, government agencies, nations, and international organizations to identify international environmental issues and to implement technical and policy responses. Coordinates an EPA-wide effort to strengthen public health and environmental protection for American Indian tribes and helps them administer their own environmental programs.
Office of Research and Development	Supports six research programs that identify environmental health research needs with input from EPA offices, partners, and stakeholders. Conducts research with three national laboratories, four national centers, and two offices located in 14 facilities.
Office of Solid Waste and Emergency Response	Provides policy, guidance, and direction for emergency response and waste programs. Develops guidelines for the land disposal of hazardous waste and provides technical assistance to all levels of government for safe practices in waste management. Supports state and local governments in redeveloping and reusing potentially contaminated sites. Manages the Comprehensive Environmental Response, Compensation, and Liability Act of 1980, also known as Superfund[a] programs for abandoned and active hazardous waste sites, and accidental oil and chemical releases. Encourages technologies to address contaminated soil and groundwater.
Office of Water	Ensures drinking water is safe, restores and maintains oceans, watersheds, and aquatic ecosystems to protect human health, support economic and recreational activities, and provide healthy habitats. Works with other federal agencies, state and local governments, American Indian tribes, and the public. Implements related laws.

Source: EPA data.

[a]The Comprehensive Environmental Response, Compensation, and Liability Act of 1980, 42 U.S.C. § 9601 et seq.

EPA's regional offices are responsible for the execution of agency programs within the states, and within some regions, including U.S. territories. Figure 1 shows the distribution of these ten regions.

Figure 1: EPA Regions

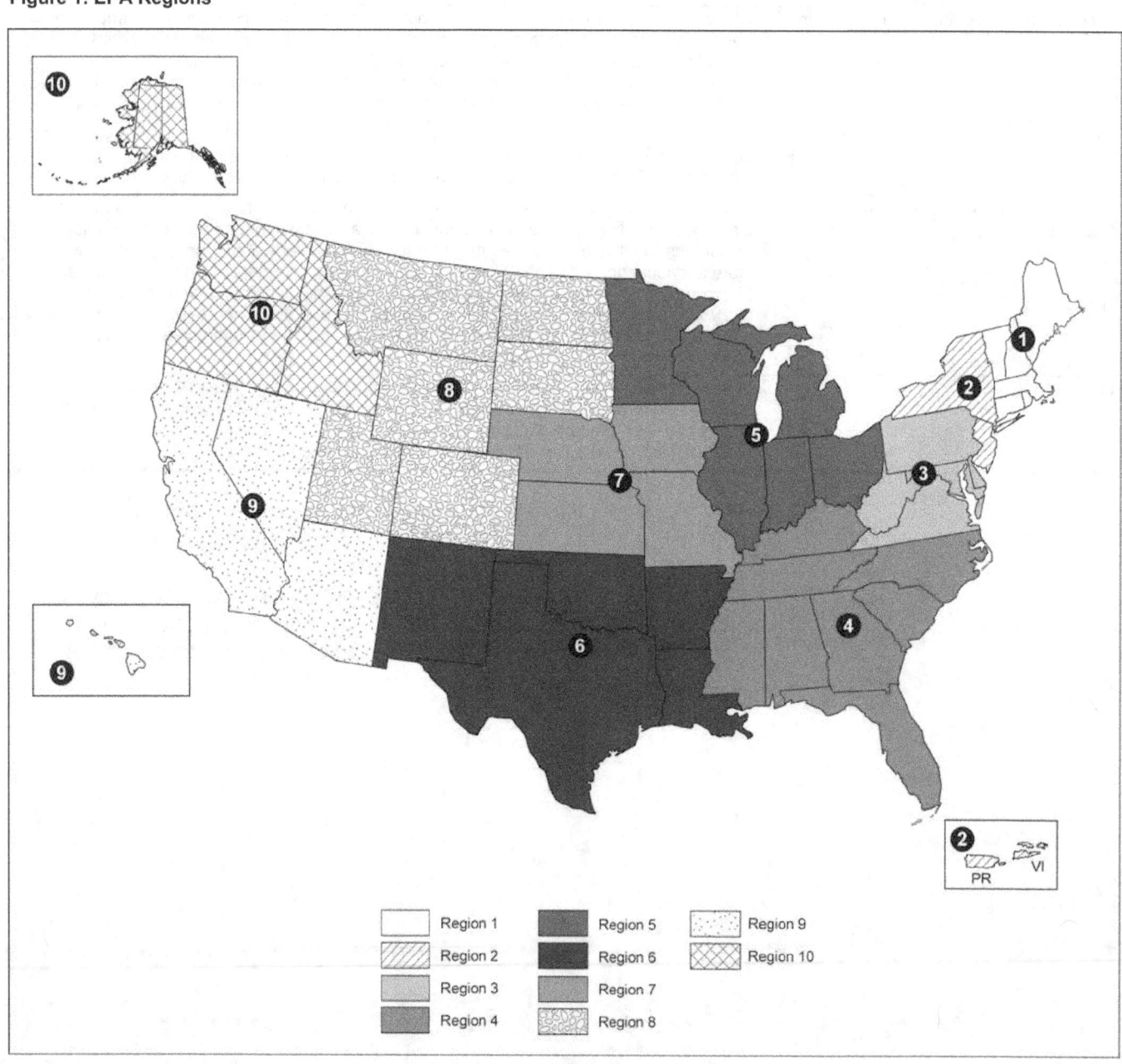

Sources: GAO analysis of EPA data; Map Resources (map).

Note: Two territories are included in this map—Puerto Rico and the U.S. Virgin Islands. Several other territories that are part of Region 9 do not appear here: American Samoa, Commonwealth of the Northern Mariana Islands, Federated States of Micronesia, Guam, Marshall Islands, and the Republic of Palau.

Secure Information Technology Is Vital to EPA's Mission

EPA relies on IT to support its mission and achieve its goals. In fiscal year 2011, the agency reported having 117 agency-operated systems and 12 contractor-operated systems. These systems include networks, telecommunications, and specific applications. The Office of Technology Operations and Planning within the Office of Environmental Information provides centralized management and control of EPA's IT resources and services, including the EPA wide area network, a primary general support system of EPA. The Office of Technology Operations and Planning is located in Washington, D.C., and provides connectivity to EPA program offices, regional offices and laboratories, and federal agencies. It is responsible for the planning, design, operation, management, and maintenance of the EPA wide area network with support from on-site contractors and its Managed Trusted Internet Protocol Services (MTIPS)[1] service provider. Two divisions within the Office of Technology Operations and Planning have primary responsibility for carrying out day-to-day operations of these services: the National Computer Center (NCC), located in Research Triangle Park, North Carolina, is responsible for EPA's wide area network operations and server operations for systems operated in the NCC. The Enterprise Desktop Solutions Division, located in Washington, D.C., is responsible for the D.C. area local area network, voice, and shared server room operation. Figure 2 depicts a simplified version of EPA's network.

---

[1]MTIPS is designed to reduce the number of Internet connections in government networks while providing security services to all government users. The General Services Administration and the Department of Homeland Security have developed the requirements for a Networx Trusted Internet Connection Access Provider service. The goal is to use Networx contracts to simplify and supplement the delivery of Trusted Internet Connections solutions to government customers as a managed security service.

Figure 2: Simplified Diagram of EPA Network

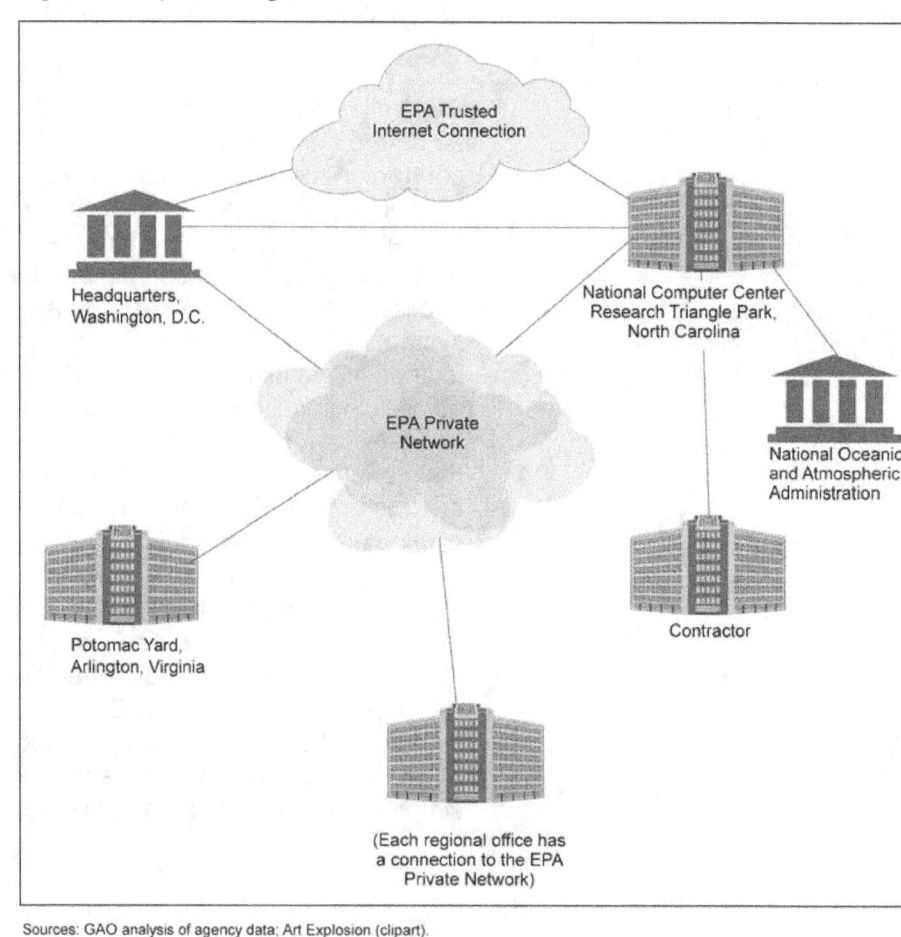

Sources: GAO analysis of agency data; Art Explosion (clipart).

EPA, in response to the Office of Management and Budget's (OMB) "Cloud First"[2] policy that requires each agency to identify three services that it will migrate to a cloud by June 2012, has identified two cloud services: Enterprise Service Desk and MTIPS, which is part of the Networx program offered by the General Services Administration. EPA also operates a virtual hosting infrastructure in four internal data centers

---

[2]Vivek Kundra, *25 Point Implementation Plan to Reform Federal Information Technology Management* (Washington, D.C.: Dec. 9, 2010).

with a standardized platform supporting up to 1,750 servers. Officials stated that the goal is to migrate e-mail and collaboration services to a commercial external cloud provider by 2015.

Responsibilities for EPA's Information Security Program

The Federal Information Security Management Act of 2002 (FISMA) requires each federal agency to develop, document, and implement an agencywide information security program to provide security for the information and information systems that support the operations and assets of the agency, including those provided or managed by other agencies, contractors, or other sources. According to FISMA, each agency is responsible for providing information security protections, commensurate with risk, for information collected or maintained by or on behalf of the agency, and information systems used or operated by the agency or on its behalf. FISMA requires that a chief information officer or a comparable official of the agency be responsible for developing and maintaining an agencywide information security program.

The Administrator of EPA is responsible for ensuring that an information security program is implemented, and that security processes are integrated with strategic and operational planning. EPA is responsible for reporting annually to congressional committees, GAO, and to the Director of OMB on the effectiveness of the agency's information security program and compliance with FISMA.[3] The Chief Information Officer appoints a senior agency information security officer and ensures that EPA's information security program follows applicable federal laws. Senior leaders of EPA's program offices and regions appoint information security officers to implement agency information security program requirements for the systems and information under their control.

The Office of Environmental Information centrally administers EPA's information security program. The Assistant Administrator of the Office of Environmental Information serves as the Chief Information Officer for EPA. As described in table 2, EPA has designated key roles in IT security according to FISMA and agency policy.

---

[3]FISMA requires each federal agency to report to specified congressional committees, GAO, and the Director of OMB each year on agency compliance with the act's information security requirements. FISMA was enacted as title III, E-Government Act of 2002, Pub. L. No.107-347, 116 Stat. 2899, 2946 (Dec. 17, 2002).

Table 2: Positions with Key Security Responsibilities in the Office of Environmental Information

Position	Key Responsibilities
Chief Information Officer	Develops and maintains the EPA-wide information security program, the network security infrastructure, and agency policies and procedures. Ensures policies and procedures address federal policies and standards.
Office of Technology Operations and Planning Office Director	Serves as the agency's chief technology officer. Communicates, develops, and issues standard operating procedures and guidance for EPA's network. Also ensures that appropriate risk and threat information is exchanged with senior agency officials.
Senior Agency Information Security Officer	Ensures compliance with overarching agency policies and federal regulations. Serves as a liaison to the agency's information security community, including key senior agency officials.
Senior Information Official	Ensures effective processes and procedures and other directives as necessary are established to implement the policies, procedures, control techniques, and other countermeasures identified under the EPA information security program and enforced within the respective office or regions. Carries out the duties of the authorizing official for the office or region. Serves as a delegated authority for information and IT management within the organization.
Computer Security Incident Response Center	Develops standard operating procedures to minimize, contain, and communicate computer incidents and ensures threat and incident information is reported. Cooperates with security and investigation authorities, including the Inspector General, and ensures prompt response to and documentation of all computer incidents.
Information System Security Officer	Supports the senior information official, system owner, and information security officer in managing and implementing the activities, processes, policies, procedures, control techniques, and other countermeasures identified under the EPA information security program and ensures protection measures are compliant with FISMA and related information security directives for the information, information system, and service assigned. Assists with developing and updating system security documentation and coordinates changes to the system. Serves as primary point of contact during an incident involving their assigned information system and reports unresolved security issues to the information security officer or system manager.
Information System Owner and Manager	Ensures that security controls implemented on their systems support management, operational, and technical requirements in agency policies and chief technology officer-issued procedures, standards, and operating practices. Updates, develops, and maintains system security documentation. Reviews and reports on the level of compliance with agency policies, procedures, and standards as required.
Information Security Officer	Supports the assistant administrator or regional administrator by managing activities identified under the EPA information security program and ensures protection measures are compliant with FISMA and related information security directives for the information, information systems, and services for their office or region. Supports the senior information official in ensuring effective processes and procedures and other directives are established as necessary to implement the policies, procedures, control techniques, and other countermeasures identified under the EPA Information Security Program and are enforced for their office or region. Coordinates and disseminates Computer Security Incident Response Center and risk management information and ensures related procedures are implemented.
Information Management Officer	Implements and administers network security policies within the organization. Ensures network security policies, procedures, and standards are fully documented and considered in the organization's information security program and acquisition efforts.

Position	Key Responsibilities
Director, Office of Administration and Resources Management	Develops, implements, and monitors EPA's physical and personnel security programs and establishes and implements related physical security standards, guidance, and procedures in accordance with EPA information security and federal physical security policies.

Source: EPA.

Control Weaknesses Threaten Information and Systems Supporting EPA's Mission

Although EPA has taken steps to safeguard the information and systems that support its mission, security control weaknesses pervade its systems and networks, thereby jeopardizing the agency's ability to sufficiently protect the confidentiality, integrity, and availability of its information and systems. These deficiencies include those related to access controls, as well as other controls such as configuration management and sensitive media protection. A key reason for these weaknesses is that EPA has not yet fully implemented its agencywide information security program to ensure that controls are appropriately designed and operating effectively. As a result, EPA has limited assurance that its information and information systems are being adequately protected against unauthorized access, use, disclosure, modification, disruption, or loss.

EPA Did Not Fully Implement Access Controls

A basic management objective for any organization is to protect the resources that support its critical operations from unauthorized access. Agencies accomplish this objective by designing and implementing controls that are intended to prevent, limit, and detect unauthorized access to computing resources, programs, information, and facilities. Inadequate access controls diminish the reliability of computerized information and increase the risk of unauthorized disclosure, modification, and destruction of sensitive information and disruption of service. Access controls include those related to (1) protection of system boundaries, (2) user identification and authentication, (3) authorization, (4) cryptography, (5) audit and monitoring, and (6) physical security.

EPA Did Not Always Protect Network Boundaries

Boundary protection controls logical connectivity into and out of networks and controls connectivity to and from devices connected to the network. For example, multiple firewalls can be deployed to prevent both outsiders and trusted insiders from gaining unauthorized access to systems, and intrusion detection technologies can be deployed to defend against attacks from the Internet. Unnecessary connectivity to an organization's network increases not only the number of access paths that must be managed and the complexity of the task, but also the risk of unauthorized access in a shared environment. National Institute of Standards and

Technology (NIST) guidance states that agencies should provide adequate protection for networks and employ information control policies and enforcement mechanisms to control the flow of information between designated sources and destinations within information systems.[4]

EPA has established network boundaries, but did not always adequately enforce those boundaries to secure connectivity into and out of its networks. For example, at one location, network boundaries did not have adequate segregation between a public library and the EPA facilities in Research Triangle Park, North Carolina. In addition, EPA had allowed unrestricted inbound use of an encrypted protocol that could be used to access EPA internal networks. As a result, EPA's networks were vulnerable to unnecessary and potentially undetectable access at these points.

EPA Users Were Not Always Properly Identified and Authenticated

A computer system must be able to identify and authenticate different users so that activities on the system can be linked to a specific individual. When an organization assigns a unique user account to a specific user, the system is able to distinguish that user from another—a process called identification. The system must also establish the validity of a user's claimed identity by requesting some kind of information, such as a password, that is known only by the user—a process known as authentication. The combination of identification and authentication—such as a user account/password combination—provides the basis for establishing individual accountability and for controlling access to the system. NIST 800-53 recommends that information systems uniquely identify and authenticate all users (or processes on behalf of users) and that systems establish complex passwords to reduce the likelihood of a successful attack. NIST also recommends using multifactor authentication to access user accounts via a network.[5]

While EPA has developed an interim security policy that addresses identification and authentication and a draft procedure that is based on NIST guidance, the agency did not always adequately implement these

---

[4]NIST, *Recommended Security Controls for Federal Information Systems and Organizations*, Special Publication 800-53 Revision 3 (Gaithersburg, Md.: August 2009).

[5]NIST defines multifactor authentication as authentication using two or more factors to achieve authentication. Factors include: (1) something you know (e.g., password or personal identification number); (2) something you have (e.g., cryptographic identification device or token); or (3) something you are (e.g., biometric).

interim requirements. For example, EPA did not authenticate routing protocols on several of its internal network devices, leaving them vulnerable. In addition, EPA did not enforce its own password complexity requirements or change passwords for multiple servers. Further, EPA did not require two-factor authentication for remote authentication and access to e-mail accounts. As a result, EPA's networks and systems are at increased risk that an unauthorized individual could guess a legitimate user's identification and password combination and gain access to these devices.

Authorization Controls Were Not Fully Implemented

Authorization is the process of granting or denying access rights and permissions to a protected resource, such as a network, a system, an application, a function, or a file. For example, operating systems have some built-in authorization features such as permissions for files and folders. Network devices, such as routers, have access control lists that can be used to authorize a user who can access and perform certain actions on the device. A key component of granting or denying access rights is the concept of "least privilege." Least privilege is a basic principle for securing computer resources and information. This principle means that a user is granted only those access rights and permissions needed to perform official duties. To restrict legitimate user access to only those programs and files needed to perform work, agencies establish access rights and permissions. "User rights" are allowable actions that can be assigned to a user or to a group of users. File and directory permissions are rules that regulate which users can access a particular file or directory and the extent of that access. To avoid unintentionally authorizing user access to sensitive files and directories, an agency must give careful consideration to its assignment of rights and permissions.

NIST requires federal agencies to grant a user only the access and rights to information and information systems needed to perform official duties. National Security Agency (NSA) network security best practice guidance recommends prohibiting root from logging directly into a remote system. The guidance also recommends creating a set of filtering rules, also known as an access control list, which permits the traffic identified on the list and prohibits other traffic.

Although EPA has established an access control methodology based on least privilege and need-to-know principles, it did not always limit user access rights and permissions to only those necessary to perform official duties. For example, EPA allowed for a large number of unused accounts across several network domains. At one location, EPA did not have adequate restrictions on a sensitive server to control access in managing and administering network devices either locally or remotely, leaving them vulnerable. In addition, EPA had not removed the accounts of former employees. The result of these weaknesses is an increased risk of unauthorized access to EPA systems and information.

EPA Did Not Always Effectively Encrypt Certain Sensitive Information

Cryptography underlies many of the mechanisms used to enforce the confidentiality and integrity of critical and sensitive information. Cryptographic tools help control access to information by making it unintelligible to unauthorized users and by protecting the integrity of transmitted or stored information. A basic element of cryptography is encryption. Encryption is the conversion of data into a form, called a cipher text, which cannot be easily understood. Encryption can be used to provide basic data confidentiality and integrity by transforming plain text into cipher text using a special value known as a key and a mathematical process known as an algorithm. NIST guidelines state that agencies should use encryption to protect the confidentiality of remote access sessions and encrypt sessions between host systems. The NIST standard for an encryption algorithm is Federal Information Processing Standards (FIPS) 140-2.[6]

EPA did not always effectively encrypt certain sensitive information. For example, EPA did not always encrypt private keys stored on certain servers and had used a weak password encryption feature on network devices. In addition, the agency allowed the use of insecure network protocols to manage network devices. The agency also did not always use a FIPS-compliant algorithm to encrypt passwords on three support servers we reviewed. These weaknesses expose critical and sensitive information to unnecessary risk of unauthorized access, modification, or destruction.

EPA Did Not Effectively Log and Monitor System Activity

To establish individual accountability, monitor compliance with security policies, and investigate security violations, it is crucial to determine what, when, and by whom specific actions have been taken on a system. Agencies accomplish this by implementing system or security software that provides an audit trail, or a log of system activity, that can be used to determine the source of a transaction or attempted transaction and to monitor a user's activities. Audit and monitoring involves the regular

---

[6]NIST, *Security Requirements for Cryptographic Modules*, FIPS 140-2 (Gaithersburg, Md.: May 2001).

collection, review, and analysis of auditable events for indications of inappropriate or unusual activity, and the appropriate investigation and reporting of such activity. Automated mechanisms may be used to integrate audit monitoring, analysis, and reporting into an overall process for investigation and response to suspicious activities. Audit and monitoring controls can help security professionals routinely assess computer security, perform investigations during and after an attack, and even recognize an ongoing attack. Audit and monitoring technologies include network and host-based intrusion detection systems, audit logging, security event correlation tools, and computer forensics.

NIST guidance states that agencies should retain sufficient audit logs to allow monitoring of key activities, provide support for after-the-fact investigation of security incidents, and meet organizational information retention requirements.

Although EPA has many useful mechanisms at its disposal to help prevent and respond to security breaches, such as firewalls and intrusion detection systems, it has not consistently implemented integrated and responsive audit and monitoring. For example, EPA had not enabled auditing on a server used for receiving confidential data from commercial entities. Furthermore, more than 150 of EPA's network devices had remote logging set to a severity level that was not sufficient for logging important security information. In addition, the number of error logs on one server database system was set so low that old logs would be overwritten as soon as this number was reached, thus removing the old logs from use. As a result, EPA is limited in its ability to establish accountability, ensure compliance with security policies, and investigate violations.

EPA Did Not Always Implement Physical Controls

Physical security controls are a key component of limiting unauthorized access to sensitive information and information systems. These controls are important for protecting computer facilities and resources from espionage, sabotage, damage, and theft. They involve restricting physical access to computer resources and sensitive information, usually by limiting access to the buildings and rooms in which the resources are housed and periodically reviewing access rights granted to ensure that access continues to be appropriate based on established criteria. Such controls include perimeter fencing; surveillance cameras; security guards; gates; locks; environmental controls such as smoke detectors, fire alarms and extinguishers; and uninterruptible power supplies. NIST guidance states that federal agencies should implement physical security and environmental safety controls to protect employees and contractors, information systems, and the facilities in which they are located.

EPA had implemented numerous physical security controls for protecting its information, information systems, and employees. For example, the agency used electronic badges, guards, magnetometers, and x-ray machines to help control access to computing environments at two locations. EPA had also implemented environmental and safety controls such as temperature and humidity controls as well as emergency lighting to protect its staff and sensitive IT resources.

Nonetheless, EPA did not always ensure that these controls were consistently implemented. For example, over a period of 5 days, five staff members at one location used their electronic badges to gain access to the computer room, but they were not on the list of staff authorized to enter the area. Two of these staff members were contractors, and the other three were EPA staff. Similarly, EPA did not always effectively control access to sensitive IT equipment kept in server or telecommunication rooms. To illustrate, visitor logs were incomplete for several rooms that contained sensitive IT equipment. These logs did not always include information such as the visitor's purpose for visiting the room, the time of departure, or the type of identification used to sign in. As a result, EPA has diminished assurance that its computing resources are protected from inadvertent or deliberate misuse including sabotage, vandalism, theft, and destruction. EPA officials stated that the access controls list issue had been resolved and that IT equipment in the rooms would be moved as part of its data center consolidation effort. The agency also provided a subsequent response stating that most of the IT equipment had been moved. We have not yet verified this information.

EPA Did Not Effectively Implement Other Controls

In addition to access controls, other important controls should be in place to ensure the confidentiality, integrity, and availability of an agency's information. These controls include policies, procedures, and techniques for securely configuring information systems, sufficiently disposing of media, and implementing personnel security. Weaknesses in these areas increase the risk of unauthorized use, disclosure, modification, or loss of sensitive information and information systems supporting EPA's mission. EPA had personnel security controls in place.

Configuration Management Controls Were Not Always Implemented

Configuration management controls ensure that only authorized and fully tested software is placed in operation, software and hardware are updated, patches are applied to these systems to protect against known vulnerabilities, and changes are documented and approved. To protect against known vulnerabilities, effective procedures must be in place, appropriate software installed, and patches updated promptly. Up-to-date patch installation helps mitigate flaws in software code that could be exploited to cause significant damage and enable malicious individuals to read, modify, or delete sensitive information or disrupt operations. NIST guidance states that agencies should document approved system changes and retain records of configuration changes to systems[7] and that agencies should configure security settings to the most restrictive mode consistent with operational requirements. Both NIST and NSA guidance recommend that certain system services be disabled.

EPA has developed, documented, and established procedures to manage configuration changes. For example, although the agencywide configuration management procedure is still a draft document, EPA's Office of Technology Operations and Planning has developed, documented, and implemented a change management process and procedures document that is intended to provide formal and standardized processes and procedures for identifying, assessing, approving, implementing, and accounting for changes to EPA information systems. In addition, the agency uses a central tool to request, approve, and track the status of configuration change requests. The system owners or managers have responsibility for documenting these changes. According to agency officials, EPA uses an automated tool for applying patches that are intended to correct software security vulnerabilities.

Despite these efforts, EPA had not always implemented configuration management controls. For example, although the agency has an automated tool in place for managing changes, officials could only provide records of approved changes for four of the six systems we reviewed. Information for the other two systems consisted only of e-mails describing the changes. Furthermore, information for only two of the six systems included the unique change request number generated by the tool; this number could be used to research and determine whether a change had been formally approved. During a demonstration of the tool, an EPA official suggested that we contact system owners for system-specific change reports. However, change information provided by the system owners varied in content, and the agencywide configuration

---

[7]NIST, Special Publication 800-53.

management guide did not instruct them on how such records should be documented.

Similarly, EPA had not securely configured its networks and databases in accordance with NIST guidance and web applications and operating systems were not always configured to the most restrictive settings in accordance with NIST guidance. Moreover, some EPA information systems and network devices were running outdated software that was no longer supported by the manufacturer, resulting in EPA being unable to effectively patch them for vulnerabilities. In addition, newly released security patches, service packs, and hot fixes had not been installed in a timely manner, and several critical systems had not been patched or were out of date, and some had known vulnerabilities. Without adequate security controls, EPA systems are susceptible to many known vulnerabilities.

EPA Did Not Always Implement Media Protection Controls

The destruction of media and their disposal are key to ensuring the confidentiality of information. Media can include magnetic tapes, optical disks (such as compact disks), and hard drives. Agencies safeguard used media to ensure that the information they contain is appropriately controlled or disposed of. Media that are improperly disposed of can lead to the inappropriate or inadvertent disclosure of an agency's sensitive information, including the personally identifiable information of its employees and customers. NIST guidance[8] states that verifying the selected information sanitization and disposal process and testing of media is an essential step for maintaining confidentiality. EPA has documented a media protection policy through its interim network security policy that states that all IT resources scheduled for disposal must be adequately sanitized to protect the confidentiality of agency information and that appropriate security controls such as those prescribed by NIST must be applied. EPA has a supplemental disk sanitization procedure, and program offices have the option to develop their own separate procedures if needed.

However, EPA did not provide evidence that equipment used for disposal of sensitive information had been tested to ensure that it was working properly. Specifically, EPA could not provide documentation or support to

---

[8]NIST *Guidelines for Media Sanitization*, Special Publication 800-88 (Gaithersburg, Md.: September 2006), provides guidance on appropriate sanitization equipment, techniques, and procedures.

verify whether or not media disposal equipment had been tested for three systems. Additionally, both sanitized and unsanitized hard drives were being kept together in the storage area for one system. None of the drives were labeled to show whether or not they had been sanitized, which could allow intended or unintended access to sensitive data on an unsanitized hard drive. Until EPA tests, documents, and implements information security controls for media disposal and sanitization, increased risk exist that the agency's sensitive information may not be adequately protected.

Personnel Security Controls Were In Place

The greatest harm or disruption to a system comes from the actions, both intentional and unintentional, of individuals. These intentional and unintentional actions can be reduced through the implementation of personnel security controls. According to NIST guidance, personnel security controls help agencies ensure that individuals occupying positions of responsibility (including third-party service providers) are trustworthy and meet established security criteria for these positions. According to NIST, personnel security controls include, among other things, that the agency develop a formal personnel security policy and screen individuals prior to authorizing access to an information system.[9] EPA's security policy for personnel screening states that the type of investigation should be based on the sensitivity of the position and the level of public trust. According to EPA policy, all system administrative staff, including contractors, must have an adequate background check.

EPA has conducted the appropriate background investigations for all 14 employees and contractors reviewed. For one system reviewed, we verified that EPA has a process in place to track whether personnel who require access to the system have the necessary security clearances.

EPA Has Not Fully Documented and Implemented Components of Its Information Security Program

A key reason for the weaknesses in controls over EPA's information and information systems is that it has not yet fully implemented its agencywide information security program to ensure that controls were effectively established and maintained. FISMA requires each agency to develop, document, and implement an information security program that, among other things, includes

---

[9]NIST, Special Publication 800-53.

- policies and procedures that (1) are based on risk assessments, (2) cost-effectively reduce risks, (3) ensure that information security is addressed throughout the life cycle of each system, and (4) ensure compliance with applicable requirements;
- plans for providing adequate information security for networks, facilities, and systems;
- security awareness training to inform personnel of information security risks and their responsibilities in complying with agency policies and procedures, and information security training for personnel with significant security responsibilities for information security;
- periodic testing and evaluation of the effectiveness of information security policies, procedures, and practices, to be performed with a frequency depending on risk, but no less than annually, and that includes testing of management, operational, and technical controls for every system identified in the agency's required inventory of major information systems;
- a process for planning, implementing, evaluating, and documenting remedial action to address any deficiencies in its information security policies, procedures, or practices; and
- plans and procedures to ensure continuity of operations for information systems that support operations and assets of the agency.

FISMA also requires agencies to maintain and update annually an inventory of major information systems and the program requirements that apply to the information and information systems that support the operations and assets of the agency, including those provided or managed by another agency, contractor, or other source.

EPA Has an Interim Security Policy and Draft Procedures

A key element of an effective information security program is to develop, document, and implement risk-based policies, procedures, and technical standards that govern the security over an agency's computing environment. If properly implemented, policies and procedures should help reduce the risk that could come from unauthorized access or disruption of services. Developing, documenting, and implementing security policies is important because they are the primary mechanisms by which management communicates its views and requirements; these policies also serve as the basis for adopting specific procedures and technical controls. In addition, agencies need to take the actions necessary to effectively implement or execute these procedures and controls. Otherwise, agency systems and information will not receive the protection that the security policies and controls should provide. FISMA requires agencies to develop and implement policies and procedures that support an effective information security program.

Although EPA has developed information security policies and procedures, most of its agencywide requirements were not finalized. For example, EPA's agencywide information security policy and its security assessment and authorization procedure are both interim documents. While EPA has developed 18 procedures that correspond to NIST's "18 families of controls,"[10] such as those for access controls, security training, and contingency planning, 17 of the procedures are still in draft, including 12 that have been in draft since 2008. The Office of Environmental Information, the organization with the primary responsibility for implementing EPA's security program, has also issued its own information security program manual intended to complement EPA's security policy. However, the Office of Environmental Information program manual has not been revised since 2006 and is not based on the current EPA interim security policy issued in August 2011.

According to EPA's Office of Environmental Information web page, the agency is undertaking an extensive IT/management policy review and update, but the website does not cite any specific dates for completion. Until EPA has finalized and implemented its security policies and procedures, the agency cannot be sure that its information security requirements are being applied consistently and effectively across the agency.

System Security Plans Referenced Outdated Policies and Procedures

An objective of system security planning is to improve the protection of IT resources. A system security plan provides an overview of the systems' security requirements and describes the controls that are in place or planned to meet those requirements. OMB Circular A-130 directs agencies to develop system security plans for major applications and general support systems, and to ensure that those plans address policies and procedures for providing management, operational, and technical controls.[11] In addition, OMB's fiscal year 2011 FISMA reporting guidance explains that agencies were expected to be in compliance with NIST

---

[10]NIST, Special Publication 800-53. NIST describes 18 control families that compose three classes of controls: management, operation, and technical controls.

[11]OMB, *Management of Federal Information Resources,* Circular No. A-130 (Washington, D.C.: Nov. 28, 2000).

standards and guidelines within 1 year of publication unless otherwise directed by OMB.[12]

EPA has developed and documented system security plans, but those plans have not been updated to reflect current policies and procedures. For example, all six systems we reviewed referenced expired policies and procedures. In addition, two of the six plans did not reflect controls identified in the current NIST Special Publication 800-53.[13] For example, two controls for moderate systems, publically accessible content and least privilege—allowing only authorized access for users—were not reflected in system security plans. An EPA official with responsibility for one of the system's that had an outdated plan attributed this to the agency not having a security procedure in place to clearly explain how updated federal guidance should be implemented. In a fiscal year 2010 report,[14] EPA's Inspector General also indentified instances where the agency's system security plans were not current.

EPA officials informed us that the agency was replacing its current automated tool for managing security with one that is intended to improve system security planning, among other activities. Currently in the pilot stage, the new tool is to provide a built-in system security planning capability and a central location to store all system security documentation. However, until EPA updates system security plans and finalizes security plan procedures, the agency may not have assurance that controls are being effectively implemented for its systems.

EPA Has Not Established a Procedure to Enforce Completion of Specialized Security Training

According to FISMA, an agencywide information security program must include security awareness training for agency personnel, contractors, and other users of information systems that support the agency's operations and assets. This training must cover (1) information security risks associated with users activities and (2) users' responsibilities in

---

[12]The 1-year compliance date for revisions to NIST publications applies only to the new and/or updated material in the publications. For information systems under development or for legacy systems undergoing significant changes, agencies are expected to be in compliance with NIST publications immediately upon deployment of the information system.

[13]NIST, Special Publication 800-53.

[14]EPA Inspector General, *Improvements Needed in Key EPA Information System Security Practices*, Report No. 10 –P-0146 (Washington D.C.: June 2010).

complying with agency policies and procedures designed to reduce these risks. FISMA also includes requirements for training personnel with significant responsibilities for information security. OMB guidance states that personnel should be trained before they are granted access to systems or applications. The training is intended to ensure that personnel are aware of the system's or application's rules, their responsibilities, and their expected behavior. In addition, EPA interim policy requires annual security awareness training to be completed by all personnel and those personnel with significant network security roles and responsibilities to complete sufficient information system security training and continuing education to ensure compliance with agency policy.

EPA has implemented a security awareness training program and maintains training records as part of its e-learning system: users of EPA systems are required to complete and pass a web-based course. According to EPA's fiscal year 2011 FISMA report, the Chief Information Officer reported that 100 percent of EPA's employees had completed the required security awareness training.

EPA also uses its e-learning system to deliver training content for employees who have significant network and system security roles. However, for this group of employees, the Chief Information Officer reported that approximately 81 percent had completed training related to their specialized security responsibilities. According to EPA officials, the agency has been unable to enforce the specialized security training requirement, which has led to reporting a lower percentage. In addition, officials also noted that formalized standard procedures related to specialized training are not well documented, including to what extent employees should complete specialized training and the specific actions to take if an employee does not complete the training.

To assist with addressing these inconsistencies, the senior agency Information Security Officer distributed a memorandum to information security officials that describes the requirement for employees with significant information security responsibilities. Specifically, EPA has determined that, at a minimum, all employees with significant security responsibilities should complete two courses using the e-learning system or through another mechanism. In addition, EPA sent e-mails to its information security officers that denote what positions include the requirement to complete the two-courses. However, EPA's actions did not ensure that all employees with significant security responsibilities met this requirement. Until EPA implements a procedure to enforce the completion of specialized security training and tailors the training to specific roles, the agency will not have reasonable assurance that its staff have the adequate knowledge, skills, and abilities consistent with their roles to protect the confidentiality of the information housed within EPA systems to which they are assigned.

EPA Did Not Document that System Controls Were Fully Tested

Another key element of an information security program is to test and evaluate policies, procedures, and controls to determine whether they are effective and operating as intended. This type of oversight is a fundamental element because it demonstrates management's commitment to the security program, reminds employees of their roles and responsibilities, and identifies and mitigates areas of noncompliance and ineffectiveness. FISMA requires that the frequency of tests and evaluations of management, operational, and technical controls be based on risks and occur no less than annually. OMB directs agencies to meet their FISMA-required controls testing by drawing on security control assessment results that include, but are not limited to, continuous monitoring activities. EPA's interim security assessment procedure requires that information system security controls be assessed annually to meet FISMA's requirements and to support continuous monitoring.

EPA had documented that management, operational, and technical controls for five of six systems were tested or reviewed. Assessment results for five systems consisted of self assessments generated by EPA's Automated System Security Evaluation and Remediation Tracking (ASSERT) tool, used for continuous monitoring, along with vulnerability assessments for two of the five systems. However, the agency did not provide any information demonstrating that controls for a clean air markets division system had been tested or reviewed at least annually. The last assessment for the system had been completed during fiscal year 2009. An EPA official stated that testing would be completed during fiscal year 2012.

We also identified data reliability challenges with EPA's ASSERT tool. The data reliability weakness with this tool was previously reported by EPA's Inspector General in 2010.[15] The Inspector General also reported in 2011 that the agency had not implemented continuous monitoring

---

[15]EPA Inspector General, *Self-reported Data Unreliable for Assessing EPA's Computer Security Program*, Report No. 10-P-0058 (Washington, D.C.: Feb. 2, 2010).

procedures or a strategy.[16] As a result, EPA has less assurance that controls over its information and information systems are adequately implemented and operating as intended.

Remedial Action Plans Were Not Reliably Documented

Remedial action plans, also known as plans of action and milestones (POA&M), help agencies identify and assess security weaknesses in information systems, set priorities, and monitor progress in correcting the weaknesses. NIST and OMB guidance specify steps that federal agencies should take to address identified security weaknesses.

- NIST standards state that organizations must periodically assess security controls in their information systems and develop and implement plans of action to correct deficiencies and reduce or eliminate vulnerabilities.
- OMB guidance specifies information that should be recorded for each POA&M, including a description of the weakness identified, the audit or other source where it was identified, and key milestones with completion dates.
- NIST guidance also states that POA&Ms should be updated to show progress made on current outstanding items and to incorporate the results of the continuous monitoring process.
- OMB guidance further states that initial milestone and completion dates should not be altered; rather, changes to dates should be recorded in a separate column.

Further, EPA procedure states that any IT security finding and recommendation that results from a review, audit, assessment, test, or from another source must be assigned a risk level and assessed for appropriate action.

EPA uses an automated tool to record and track remediation of vulnerabilities. This tool contains fields for entering a description of each weakness, where it was reported, the risk level, milestones describing appropriate actions and their completion dates, and the status of actions taken. However, the manner in which the agency uses the tool can preclude retrieval of specific POA&Ms and pose weaknesses with data reliability. For example, EPA officials were unable to locate certain

---

[16]EPA Inspector General, *Fiscal Year 2011 Federal Information Security Management Act Report: Status of EPA's Computer Security Program*, Report No. 12-P-0062 (Washington D.C.: Nov. 9, 2011).

POA&Ms pertaining to findings and recommendations in fiscal year 2011 reports from EPA, the agency's Inspector General, and GAO. These officials could not find the requested information because POA&M entries did not have all the information called for by federal guidance. In particular, these entries lacked a specific description of each weakness and did not list the report where the weakness had initially been identified. Additionally, the tool does not have built-in safeguards to keep individuals who have access to POA&Ms from altering initial milestone and completion dates. Since the Chief Information Officer and other agency officials use POA&M information to track the progress of corrective actions, inaccurate milestone information could hinder their efforts to effectively remediate program and system-level IT security weaknesses.

The EPA Inspector General had also documented weaknesses in the agency's remediation process. In its fiscal year 2011 FISMA report, the Inspector General found that EPA does not consistently create POA&Ms for vulnerabilities and the agency missed remediation deadlines for about 20 percent of the POA&Ms that have been created. Another fiscal year 2011 Inspector General report found that data in the agency's POA&M tracking tool is unreliable, and that EPA lacked the skills and resources needed to identify and remediate ongoing cyber threats.

EPA officials noted that deficiencies in the way that the current tool is used are expected to be addressed when the new remediation tool is deployed agencywide in fiscal year 2013. Until weaknesses with EPA's remediation of vulnerabilities have been resolved, they will compromise the ability of the Chief Information Officer and other EPA officials to track, assess, and report accurately the status of the agency's information security.

Contingency Plans Lacked Key Information

Contingency planning is a critical component of information protection. If normal operations are interrupted, network managers must be able to detect, mitigate, and recover from a service disruption while preserving access to vital information. Contingency plans detail emergency response, backup operations, and disaster recovery for information systems. To mitigate service disruptions, these plans should be clearly documented, communicated to potentially affected staff, updated to reflect current operations, and regularly tested. FISMA, a NIST Special Publication, and EPA procedures specify requirements and guidelines for contingency planning.

- FISMA requires each agency to develop, document, and implement plans and procedures to ensure continuity of operations for information systems that support the agency's operations and assets.
- NIST guidance states that contingency plans for information systems be developed and tested. [17] In addition, the plans should account for primary and alternate contact methods and should discuss procedures to be followed if an individual cannot be contacted.
- EPA procedures further specify that the plans must be reviewed, tested, and updated at least annually.

EPA has taken steps to implement FISMA requirements and NIST specifications but has not fully met them. Contingency plans were in place for five of the six systems we reviewed. The contingency needs for the one remaining system were addressed in disaster recovery plans. However, the agency did not follow its own procedures or NIST guidance for approving contingency plans, reviewing them annually, and updating them as necessary. All six of the plans lacked evidence that they had been signed by the approving officials. According to EPA, an approving official does not need to sign a contingency plan because the plan is included in each system's certification and authorization package and approval of the package applies to all documents within it. The agency provided documentation indicating that system security plans were part of certification and authorization packages, and two systems had contingency plans embedded in their respective system security plans. However, EPA did not provide clear evidence that contingency plans were included in certification and authorization packages for the other four systems. In addition, two of the six plans had no evidence of having had an annual review. Without clear dates for initial approvals and subsequent reviews, EPA employees and contractors cannot be certain that they have access to current, updated versions of contingency plans.

In addition to providing current information, plans are to provide adequate contact information on personnel who may be needed during an emergency. For example, the National Computer Center Hosting Systems contingency plan states that personal contact information should include home addresses, cell phone numbers, pager numbers, and alternate contact information. Among the six plans reviewed, five did not provide full contact information for some staff listed, giving only office telephone

---

[17]NIST *Contingency Planning Guide for Federal Information Systems*, Special Publication 800-34 Revision 1 (Gaithersburg, Md.: May, 2010).

numbers and e-mail addresses or, in some cases, office numbers alone. Having inadequate information could jeopardize the agency's ability to contact key personnel during an emergency.

To help ensure that contingency plans are viable and will meet an agency's needs during an emergency, these plans should be tested at least annually. While EPA provided evidence that it had tested three of the six plans in 2011, it did not provide the requested test results for the other three plans.

The EPA Inspector General has also noted deficiencies with the agency's contingency planning. In reports from fiscal years 2009 through 2011, the Inspector General described plans that lacked approval, were out of date, did not have a record of changes, and did not have evidence that contingency plans had been tested annually.[18]

Until EPA addresses identified weaknesses in its contingency planning processes, the agency will have less assurance that it can recover important systems in a timely manner when disruptions occur.

EPA Did Not Ensure that Its Inventory of Major Systems Was Accurate

FISMA requires agencies to maintain and update annually an inventory of major information systems operated by the agency or operated by others on its behalf, such as those operated by a contractor or other third party. For their fiscal year 2011 FISMA reports, agencies were required to report the number of agency and contractor systems by impact levels.[19] For fiscal year 2011, EPA reported a total of 129 systems, composed of 117 agency and 12 contractor systems, as shown by impact level in table 3. This represents a slight decrease in the total number of systems from

---

[18]U.S. Environmental Protection Agency Office of Inspector General, *EPA Has Taken Steps to Address Cyber Threats but Key Actions Remain Incomplete*, Report No. 11-P-0277 (Washington, D.C.: June 23, 2011) ; *Improvements Needed in Key EPA Information System Security Practices*, Report No. 10-P-0146 (Washington, D.C.: June 15, 2010); *Self-reported Data Unreliable for Assessing EPA's Computer Security Program*, Report No. 10-P-0058 (Washington, D.C.: Feb. 2, 2010); and *Steps Taken But More Work Needed to Strengthen Governance, Increase Utilization, and Improve Security Planning for the Exchange Network*, Report No. 09-P-0184 (Washington, D.C.: June 30, 2009).

[19]NIST Federal Information Processing Standards Publication 199, *Standards for Security Categorization of Federal Information and Information Systems*, defines three impact levels where the loss of confidentiality, integrity, or availability could be expected to have a limited adverse effect (low), a serious adverse effect (moderate), or a severe or catastrophic adverse effect (high) on organizational operations, organizational assets, or individuals.

fiscal year 2010, with the number of agency systems remaining the same and the number of contractor systems decreasing.

Table 3: EPA's Total Number of Agency and Contractor Systems in Fiscal Years 2010 and 2011 by Impact Level

	Agency		Contractor		Total	
	FY10	FY11	FY10	FY11	FY10	FY11
High	1	1	0	0	1	1
Moderate	85	87	10	8	95	95
Low	31	29	4	4	35	33
Not categorized	0	0	0	0	0	0
Total	**117**	**117**	**14**	**12**	**131**	**129**

Source: GAO analysis of EPA FISMA reports fiscal year 2010 and fiscal year 2011.

EPA did not ensure that its inventory of information systems was accurate. For example, the total number of systems in inventories provided by EPA on August 5, 2011, and September 26, 2011, did not equal each other or equal the number of systems in the agency's fiscal year 2011 FISMA report. Specifically, the initial inventory provided listed 59 general support systems and 85 major applications for a total of 144 systems, but a subsequent list reflected 47 general support systems and 85 major applications, for a total of 132 systems. Within that same time, the agency provided another listing that consisted of only general support systems; that list identified 57 general support systems, a number that did not equal the totals on either of the two inventories.

EPA also provided three lists of systems that the agency had determined contained or processed confidential business information, and all three lists differed in the number of systems identified, totaling 19, 21, and 24 systems. One system on the third list was not included on either of the first two inventories provided by EPA. Furthermore, three systems were erroneously listed twice, with minor variations of the spelling of the system names as the distinguishing information between the duplicate entries. These errors could be due to inadvertent data entry errors, as the agency places responsibility on individual information security officers to update the central systems inventory that is maintained in its ASSERT tool. The agency's Inspector General has previously identified issues with the quality of system-related information entered into the tool.

As a result, senior management has reduced assurance that the inventory accurately represents the number of EPA systems cited in its annual FISMA reporting and reduced assurance that agency information systems have been accounted for properly.

Conclusions

Although EPA has implemented numerous controls and procedures intended to protect key information and information systems, control weaknesses continue to jeopardize the confidentiality, integrity, and availability of its sensitive information. The agency has established a framework for its information security program and taken actions toward developing, documenting, and implementing the components of its program. However, there are weaknesses in access controls and other information security controls over EPA's systems. Additionally, some control deficiencies are longstanding, having been identified in past reports by the EPA Inspector General. These shortcomings will likely persist until EPA (1) addresses weaknesses such as those for identification and authentication, authorization, cryptography, audit and monitoring, physical security, and configuration management and (2) fully implements key components of a comprehensive information security program that ensures that policies and procedures are completed and effectively implemented; security plans are updated to reflect current federal and agency requirements; remedial actions are effectively managed for all weaknesses; and management, operational, and technical controls for all systems are tested and evaluated at least annually. However, until EPA fully implements these controls, it will have limited assurance that its information and information systems are being adequately protected against unauthorized access, disclosure, modification, and loss.

Recommendations for Executive Action

To help establish an effective and comprehensive information security program for EPA's information and information systems, we recommend that the Administrator of EPA direct the Assistant Administrator for the Office of Environmental Information to take the following 12 actions:

- Update configuration management procedures to ensure they include guidance for documenting records of approved changes.
- Finalize the 17 agencywide interim information security policies and draft procedures.
- Update system security plans to reflect current policies and procedures.

- Include current NIST Special Publication 800-53 guidance in system security plans.
- Develop and finalize a role-based security training procedure that tailors specific training requirements to EPA users' role/position descriptions and details the actions information security officers must take when users do not complete the training.
- Conduct testing of management, operational, and technical controls, based on risks, to occur no less than annually, for the clean air markets division system identified.
- Include features in the planned remedial action tracking tool that will require users to enter all information required by OMB policy, including descriptions of each weakness and the source of the finding.
- Include features in the planned remedial action tracking tool that block inappropriate alteration of data.
- Implement an agencywide, uniform method for approving contingency plans.
- Develop and implement procedures to annually test the viability of contingency plans for agency systems.
- Develop and implement procedures to ensure that both work and home contact information are included for each individual in a contingency plan's emergency contact list.
- Implement procedures to verify the accuracy of system inventory information.

In a separate report with limited distribution, we are also making 94 detailed recommendations to correct weaknesses in access controls and in other information security controls.

Agency Comments and Our Evaluation

In providing written comments on a draft of this report (reprinted in app. II), EPA's Assistant Administrator stated that the agency's response reflected its continued efforts to ensure that information assets are protected and secured in a manner consistent with the risk and magnitude of the harm resulting from loss, misuse, or unauthorized access to or modification of information. The Assistant Administrator also indicated that the agency agreed with 10 of our 12 draft recommendations, and partially agreed with the other 2 recommendations, as discussed below.

- EPA agreed with implementing our recommendation to implement an agencywide method for approving contingency plans, but did not agree with requiring the approving officials' signature and date to be on the document. The agency stated that a centralized repository for managing all security documents would be the more appropriate mechanism for ensuring plans are the most recent official versions. We believe this alternative action meets the intent of our draft recommendation and have modified our recommendation accordingly.

- For the second recommendation, EPA agreed to implement a uniform method for recording annual contingency plan testing, but did not agree to keep records of contingency plan testing within the contingency plans. The intent of our draft recommendation was to ensure that EPA implements procedures to test contingency plans at least annually. Accordingly, we have clarified our recommendation to emphasize this point.

As agreed with your offices, unless you publicly announce the contents of this report earlier, we plan no further distribution of it until 30 days from the date of this letter. At that time, we will send copies to interested congressional committees and to the Administrator of the Environmental Protection Agency. In addition, the report will be available at no charge on the GAO website at http://www.gao.gov.

If you or your staff have any questions about this report, please contact Gregory C. Wilshusen at (202) 512-6244 or wilshuseng@gao.gov or Dr. Nabajyoti Barkakati at (202) 512-4499 or barkakatin@gao.gov. Contact points for our Offices of Congressional Relations and Public Affairs may be found on the last page of this report. Key contributors to this report are listed in appendix III.

Gregory C. Wilshusen
Director, Information Security Issues

Dr. Nabajyoti Barkakati
Chief Technologist

List of Requesters

The Honorable Fred Upton
Chairman
The Honorable Henry A. Waxman
Ranking Member
Committee on Energy and Commerce
House of Representatives

The Honorable Ed Whitfield
Chairman
The Honorable Bobby L. Rush
Ranking Member
Subcommittee on Energy and Power
Committee on Energy and Commerce
House of Representatives

The Honorable John Shimkus
Chairman
The Honorable Gene Green
Ranking Member
Subcommittee on Environment and the Economy
Committee on Energy and Commerce
House of Representatives

The Honorable Greg Walden
Chairman
The Honorable Anna G. Eshoo
Ranking Member
Subcommittee on Communications and Technology
Committee on Energy and Commerce
House of Representatives

Appendix I: Objective, Scope, and Methodology

The objective of our review was to determine whether the Environmental Protection Agency (EPA) had effectively implemented appropriate information security controls to protect the confidentiality, integrity, and availability of the information and systems that support its mission.

To determine the effectiveness of EPA's security controls, we gained an understanding of the overall network control environment, identified interconnectivity and control points, and examined controls for the agency's networks and facilities. Specifically, we reviewed controls over EPA's network infrastructure and systems that support EPA's business functions of air, land, and water quality management and process or contain confidential business information. We performed our work at EPA's National Computer Center in Research Triangle Park, North Carolina; Potomac Yard Data Center in Arlington, Virginia; and at EPA headquarters in Washington, D.C. We selected these sites to maximize audit coverage while limiting travel costs, since the majority of EPA systems and applications are supported or maintained in these locations.

We used GAO's Federal Information System Controls Audit Manual, which contains guidance for reviewing information system controls that affect the confidentiality, integrity, and availability of computerized information;[1] National Institute of Standards and Technology (NIST) standards and guidance; and EPA's policies, procedures, practices, and standards to evaluate the agency's controls over its information systems. Specifically, we

- reviewed network access paths to determine if boundaries had been adequately protected;
- reviewed the complexity and expiration of password settings to determine if password management was being enforced;
- analyzed users' system authorizations to determine whether they had more permissions than necessary to perform their assigned functions;
- observed methods for providing secure data transmissions across the network to determine whether sensitive data were being encrypted;
- reviewed software security settings to determine if modifications of sensitive or critical system resources had been monitored and logged;

---

[1]GAO, *Federal Information System Controls Audit Manual (FISCAM)*, GAO-09-232G (Washington, D.C.: February 2009).

- observed physical access controls to determine if computer facilities
  and resources were being protected from espionage, sabotage,
  damage, and theft;
- examined configuration settings and access controls for routers,
  network management servers, switches, and firewalls;
- inspected key servers and workstations to determine if critical patches
  had been installed and/or were up-to-date;
- reviewed media handling procedures to determine if equipment used
  for clearing sensitive data had been tested to ensure correct
  performance; and
- reviewed personnel clearance procedures to determine whether staff
  had been properly cleared prior to gaining access to sensitive
  information or information systems.

Using the requirements identified by the Federal Information Security
Management Act of 2002 (FISMA), which establishes key elements for an
effective agencywide information security program, and associated NIST
guidelines and EPA requirements, we evaluated EPA systems and
networks by

- analyzing EPA policies, procedures, practices, and standards to
  determine their effectiveness in providing guidance to personnel
  responsible for securing information and information systems;
- analyzed security plans for six systems to determine if those plans
  had been documented and updated according to federal guidance;
- examined the security awareness training process for employees and
  contractors to determine whether they had received training according
  to federal requirements;
- examined training records for personnel who have significant
  responsibilities to determine whether they had received training
  commensurate with those responsibilities;
- analyzed EPA's procedures and results for testing and evaluating
  security controls to determine whether management, operational, and
  technical controls for six systems had been sufficiently tested at least
  annually and based on risk;
- reviewed EPA's implementation of continuous monitoring and use of
  automated tools to determine the extent to which it uses these tools to
  manage IT assets and monitor the security configurations and
  vulnerabilities for its IT assets;
- evaluated EPA's process to correct weaknesses and determine
  whether remedial action plans complied with federal guidance; and

- examined contingency plans for six systems to determine whether those plans had been developed and tested.

We also discussed with key security representatives and management officials whether information security controls were in place, adequately designed, and operating effectively.

To determine the reliability of EPA's computer-processed data, we performed an assessment. We evaluated the materiality of the data to our audit objectives and assessed the data by various means, including reviewing related documents, interviewing knowledgeable agency officials, and reviewing internal controls. Through a combination of methods, we concluded that the data were sufficiently reliable for the purposes of our work.

We conducted this performance audit from July 2011 to July 2012 in accordance with generally accepted government auditing standards. Those standards require that we plan and perform the audit to obtain sufficient, appropriate evidence to provide a reasonable basis for our findings and conclusions based on our audit objective. We believe that the evidence obtained provides a reasonable basis for our findings and conclusions based on our audit objective.

Appendix II: Comments from the Environmental Protection Agency

UNITED STATES ENVIRONMENTAL PROTECTION AGENCY
WASHINGTON, D.C. 20460

OFFICE OF
ENVIRONMENTAL INFORMATION

Mr. Gregory C. Wilshusen
Director, Information Technology Team
Government Accountability Office
Washington, DC 20548

Dear Mr. Wilshusen:

Thank you for the opportunity to comment on the Government Accountability Office (GAO) draft report GAO-12-696 entitled "*INFORMATION SECURITY Environmental Protection Agency Needs to Resolve Weaknesses.*" I am forwarding Environmental Protection Agency's (EPA) response on behalf of the Office of Environmental Information (OEI) as well as the other EPA program offices involved. We agree with the recommendations with the exceptions as noted in our enclosed response.

Our response reflects EPA's continued efforts to ensure that information assets are protected and secured in a manner consistent with the risk and magnitude of the harm resulting from the loss, misuse, or unauthorized access to or modification of information.

If you have any questions or concerns regarding this response to the recommendations, please feel free to contact Robert McKinney at (202) 564-0921.

Sincerely,

Malcolm Jackson
Assistant Administrator

Enclosure

Internet Address (URL) ● http://www.epa.gov
Recycled/Recyclable ● Printed with Vegetable Oil Based Inks on 100% Postconsumer, Process Chlorine Free Recycled Paper

cc: Betsy Shaw, OAR
      John Showman, OARM
      Renee Wynn, OEI
      Marylouise Uhlig, OCSPP
      Nigel Simon, OSWER
      Mike Shapiro, OW

Enclosure: EPA Response to Government Accountability Office (GAO) draft report GAO-12-696 entitled
INFORMATION SECURITY Environmental Protection Agency Needs to Resolve Weaknesses

Recommendation 1: Update configuration management procedures to ensure it includes guidance for documenting records of approved changes.

EPA agrees with recommendation and is in the process of configuration management procedures accordingly.

Recommendation 2: Finalize the 17 agencywide interim information security policies and draft procedures.

EPA agrees with recommendation and expects to finalize and publish new policy and associated interim procedures by end of July 2012.

Recommendation 3: Update system security plans to reflect current policies and procedures.

EPA agrees with recommendation and will update system security plans accordingly.

Recommendation 4: Include current NIST Special Publication 800-53 guidance in system security plans.

EPA agrees with recommendation and will update system security plans to reflect current 800-53 guidance.

Recommendation 5: Develop and finalize a role-based security training procedure that tailors specific training requirements to EPA users' role/position descriptions and details the actions information security officers must take when users do not complete the training.

EPA agrees with recommendation and will continue coordinating with EPA Office of Inspector General to analyze EPA roles and responsibilities for personnel with significant security responsibilities. EPA will develop and implement tailored role based training based on the analyses. Related procedures will be documented in a procedure as part of effort discussed for Recommendation 2.

Recommendation 6: Conduct testing of management, operational, and technical controls, at least annually for system identified.

EPA agrees with recommendation and will continue with transition to third party annual assessments for moderate and high categorized systems across EPA started in October 2011.

Recommendation 7: Include features in the planned remedial action tracking tool that will require users to enter all information required by OMB policy, including descriptions of each weakness and the source of the finding.

EPA agrees with recommendation and is scheduled to complete transition to planned remedial action tracking tool by October 2012 to address shortcomings of current tool.

Recommendation 8: Include features in the planned remedial action tracking tool that block inappropriate alteration of data.

EPA agrees with recommendation and is scheduled to complete transition to planned remedial action tracking tool by October 2012 to address shortcomings of current tool.

Recommendation 9: Implement an agencywide, uniform method for approving contingency plans that follows NIST standards and includes the approving official's signature and the date of the approval on the document.

EPA partially agrees with recommendation and will implement an agencywide, uniform method for approving contingency plans that follows NIST standards. EPA does not agree that the approving official's signature and date of the approval are required on the document. In addition, initial and subsequent update dates on documents do not provide certainty that users have the most recent versions. EPA believes a centralized repository designated as the official repository where all system security documents are managed provides the appropriate certainty mechanism where users know the most recently dated document versions are officially the most recent versions. EPA is scheduled to complete transition to a centralized repository that will be the official repository for all system security documents by October 2012.

Recommendation 10: Develop and implement procedures to ensure that records of annual tests are included within contingency plans.

EPA partially agrees with recommendation and will implement an agencywide, uniform method for recording annual contingency plan testing. EPA does not agree such records need to be within the contingency plans.

Recommendation 11: Develop and implement procedures to ensure that both work and home contact information are included for each individual in a contingency plan's emergency contact lists.

EPA will include work information at a minimum and home contact information as required based on individual roles.

Recommendation 12: Implement procedures to verify the accuracy of system inventory information.

EPA agrees with recommendation and will implement procedures to verify the accuracy of system inventory information.

Appendix III: GAO Contacts and Staff Acknowledgments

GAO Contacts

Gregory C. Wilshusen, (202) 512-6244, wilshuseng@gao.gov

Dr. Nabajyoti Barkakati, (202) 512-4499, barkakatin@gao.gov

Staff Acknowledgments

In addition to the individuals named above, the following made key contributions to this report: West Coile, Anjalique Lawrence, Duc Ngo, and Chris Warweg, (assistant directors); Gary Austin; Angela Bell; Larry Crosland; Saar Dagani; Kirk Daubenspeck; Nancy Glover; Kevin Metcalfe; Mary Marshall; Sean Mays; Dana Pon; Jason Porter, Sr.; and Eugene Stevens.

GAO's Mission	The Government Accountability Office, the audit, evaluation, and investigative arm of Congress, exists to support Congress in meeting its constitutional responsibilities and to help improve the performance and accountability of the federal government for the American people. GAO examines the use of public funds; evaluates federal programs and policies; and provides analyses, recommendations, and other assistance to help Congress make informed oversight, policy, and funding decisions. GAO's commitment to good government is reflected in its core values of accountability, integrity, and reliability.
Obtaining Copies of GAO Reports and Testimony	The fastest and easiest way to obtain copies of GAO documents at no cost is through GAO's website (www.gao.gov). Each weekday afternoon, GAO posts on its website newly released reports, testimony, and correspondence. To have GAO e-mail you a list of newly posted products, go to www.gao.gov and select "E-mail Updates."
Order by Phone	The price of each GAO publication reflects GAO's actual cost of production and distribution and depends on the number of pages in the publication and whether the publication is printed in color or black and white. Pricing and ordering information is posted on GAO's website, http://www.gao.gov/ordering.htm. Place orders by calling (202) 512-6000, toll free (866) 801-7077, or TDD (202) 512-2537. Orders may be paid for using American Express, Discover Card, MasterCard, Visa, check, or money order. Call for additional information.
Connect with GAO	Connect with GAO on Facebook, Flickr, Twitter, and YouTube. Subscribe to our RSS Feeds or E-mail Updates. Listen to our Podcasts. Visit GAO on the web at www.gao.gov.
To Report Fraud, Waste, and Abuse in Federal Programs	Contact: Website: www.gao.gov/fraudnet/fraudnet.htm E-mail: fraudnet@gao.gov Automated answering system: (800) 424-5454 or (202) 512-7470
Congressional Relations	Katherine Siggerud, Managing Director, siggerudk@gao.gov, (202) 512-4400, U.S. Government Accountability Office, 441 G Street NW, Room 7125, Washington, DC 20548
Public Affairs	Chuck Young, Managing Director, youngc1@gao.gov, (202) 512-4800 U.S. Government Accountability Office, 441 G Street NW, Room 7149 Washington, DC 20548

Please Print on Recycled Paper.